CAVENDISH HERB HANDBOOKS

GARDEN
HERBS

LESLEY BREMNESS

CAVENDISH BOOKS, VANCOUVER

A CAVENDISH HERB HANDBOOK

A DORLING KINDERSLEY BOOK

Project Editor	Sara Harper
North American Editor	Mary Sutherland
Art Editor	Ann Burnham
DTP Designers	Suzy Dittmar, Paul Wood
Managing Editor	Fay Franklin
Managing Art Editor	Virginia Walter
Production Manager	Maryann Rogers

IMPORTANT NOTICE

Each herb entry may contain a caution regarding its use. Please read with care. Do not try self-diagnosis or self-treatment during pregnancy, or for serious or long-term problems, without consulting a doctor. Seek medical advice if symptoms persist.

Reprinted 1997
2 4 6 8 10 9 7 5 3

Published in Canada by
Cavendish Books Inc.
Unit 5, 801 West 1st Street,
North Vancouver BC V7P 1A4
Visit us on the World Wide Web at www.gardenbooks.com

CIP record available from National Library, Ottawa

ISBN 0-929050-78-9

Reproduced by Colorlito Rigogliosi S.r.l., Milan, Italy
Printed and bound in Italy by LEGO

CONTENTS

INTRODUCTION

Herbs, these fragrant, tasty, healing plants, have become an integral part of daily life. When they catch our interest in one area, they gently entice us into others. You may begin as an eager cook beguiled by their flavors and soon be counting their health benefits, or you may enjoy their perfume and become curious about aromatherapy. You could plant herbs for their subtle beauty and discover organic gardening.

Herbs link us with the past and the future. They carry a rich and evocative history, from Cleopatra's perfumes to the flavorings of classic cuisine, and offer enormous potential for the future, from new beauty treatments to immune system boosters.

This book shows how easy it is to cultivate herbs, whether you have a window box or a garden. The more of these horticultural treasures we grow and use, the more we realize that the plants themselves are engaging teachers. I hope you enjoy this primer on your journey of discovery.

Designing your
HERB
GARDEN

❖

*Herb gardens can be almost
any shape or size, from formal
with geometric patterns to
informal with free-flowing
lines. This section shows how
to design a herb garden, with
illustrated plans of different
styles that make the most of
the decorative and aromatic
qualities of herbs.*

PLANNING A GARDEN

If you are new to gardening, consider how much time and effort you have available before embarking on your design, and perhaps start with a small area or a few large containers. As your confidence grows, you can extend your range of these fragrant, tasty herbs into a special garden. Remember to include a bench to encourage relaxation in this tranquil place.

SELECTING A SITE

An ideal site is mostly in sun and sheltered. When choosing, note where water collects and shadows fall. Enclose with a hedge, wall, or screen to create privacy and reduce wind.

DESIGNING YOUR GARDEN

Decide if you want a formal garden, following geometric patterns, or an informal one that dictates its own shape. Measure your site and draw up the area on squared grid

Container garden *A window box is ideal for growing a selection of herbs.*

Formal garden *Contrasting colors enhance the bold, geometric design.*

paper; start with a base line measured from your house. Mark in existing features such as fences or trees and then plan paths and beds. The lush growth of herbs suits a disciplined design.

A PLANTING PLAN

Position plants in terms of how you plan to use them, such as culinary herbs by a kitchen door. Consider contrasting leaf size and color, plant shapes and heights. One plant per square foot or ten per square meter gives plenty of space for most perennials to grow. Use tall plants as focal points or as screens.

PATHS

For convenient access, herbs should be no more than 30in (75cm) from a path, giving a maximum bed width of 4–5ft (1.2–1.5m). Paths are also crucial to design for the color and patterns they can bring, as well as the way they define shape in all seasons.

MARKING OUT THE SITE

Prepare soil (pp.76–7) then, following your design, mark out the boundaries, beds, and paths with stakes. Delineate areas with string and pegs or a sprinkling of lime or sand.

Informal garden *Herbs are massed together for a natural, romantic effect.*

Aromatic garden *Roses dominate this fragrant, old-fashioned herb garden.*

A CELTIC KNOT GARDEN

This formal garden, with its clipped edges, is designed to give a sense of order, as well as easy access. The knot effect, based on a Celtic design, has been created by weaving contrasting paths of brick and grass.

GARDEN PLAN

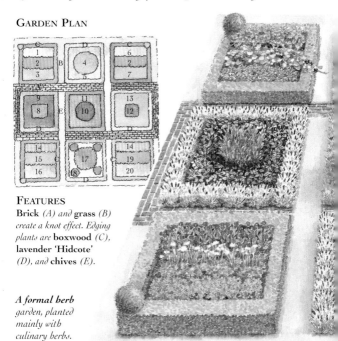

FEATURES
Brick *(A) and* **grass** *(B) create a knot effect. Edging plants are* **boxwood** *(C),* **lavender 'Hidcote'** *(D), and* **chives** *(E).*

A formal herb garden, planted mainly with culinary herbs.

10

PLANT KEY

1 Variegated lemon balm *citrus leaves*
2 Nasturtium *bright, edible flowers and leaves*
3 Coriander *pungent leaves and seeds*
4 Rosemary *resinous, needle-like leaves*
5 Borage *float blue flowers in cold drinks*
6 Marjorams *pretty, aromatic golden leaves*
7 Mints *for herbal teas*
8 French tarragon *intriguing bittersweet taste*
9 Purple basil *spicy favorite in Italian food*
10 Bay *clip into a ball*
11 Wild strawberries *delicious fleshy red fruit*
12 Dill *goes well with fish*
13 Sorrel *sharp-tasting*
14 Calendula *versatile cosmetic and culinary herb*
15 Chervil *parsley taste with a hint of myrrh*
16 Golden thymes *lemon and common types*
17 Purple sage *strong-flavored culinary herb*
18 Salad burnet *add to drinks and salads*
19 Parsley *makes an attractive garnish*
20 Gold purslane *nutty salad leaves*

Size: 20 x 20ft (6 x 6m)

AN AROMATIC GARDEN

A herb garden created for its scent is a wonderful place to linger. This one, featuring fragrant old roses, has a symmetrical design of pink/purple and white/gold beds, with the same herbs planted in opposite diagonals (any exceptions are described in brackets in the plant key). The rose-covered pergola creates peace and privacy.

FEATURES
Pergola *with 'New Dawn' roses and honeysuckle.*
Path *of 18in (45cm) peach-brown paving slabs and bricks.*

Size: approx. 28 x 20ft (8.5 x 6m)

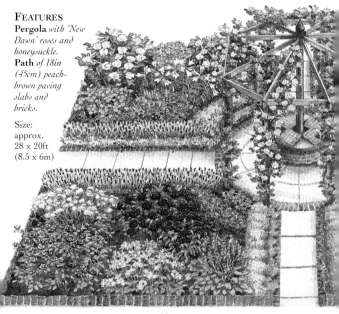

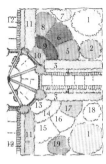

Garden Plan and Plant Key

1 Roses *'Fantin-Latour',* *'Isaac Pereire', 'Celestial', 'Blanc Double de Coubert'*

2 Purple sage *(diagonal bed has* **meadowsweet***)*

3 Lavender 'Hidcote'

4 Pinks *'Mrs Sinkins'* *(white) and a pink form*

5 Double red peony *for perfume and color*

6 Bee balm *red flowers, eau de Cologne leaves*

7 Soapwort *pink flowers,* *raspberry-cream scent*

8 Clary sage *pungent leaves, long-lasting flowers*

9 'Fragrantissimus' thyme *sweet and fruity*

10 Sweet violet *purple or white fragrant blooms*

11 Santolina *aromatic silver leaves, yellow flowers*

12 Lawn chamomile 'Treneague' *apple scent*

13 'Doone Valley' thyme *lemon aroma*

14 Golden marjoram *savory, spicy leaves*

15 Double white peony *fragrant garden flowers*

16 Madonna lily *honey-scented, waxy flowers*

17 Eau de Cologne mint *purple-tinged leaves*

18 Sweet rocket *pastel fragrant flowers (***evening primrose** *in diagonal bed)*

19 Rosemary *leaf has pine scent (diagonal bed has* **lemon balm***)*

An aromatic herb garden blends fragrance with shades of color.

A MEDICINAL GARDEN

Herbs have been used medicinally throughout history. New research confirms the value of many, but some are toxic and should be used only by qualified herbalists. Most of the herbs in this design can be used to treat minor ailments at home.

GARDEN PLAN

Size: approx. 18 x 18ft (5.5 x 5.5m)

PLANT KEY

1 Evening primrose *sprinkle crushed seed on food for premenstrual tension*
2 Wild strawberry *can soothe mild sunburn*
3 Purple sage *antiseptic leaf tea soothes sore throats*
4 Borage *leaf infusion in moderation is adrenal tonic*
5 Chamomile *flower tea for insomnia and stress*
6 Parsley *freshens breath; diuretic*
7 Rose *(apothecary's rose) gargle with a petal infusion for sore throats*
8 Thymes: common (a), 'Doone Valley '(b), caraway (c) *strong antiseptic; leaf tea for colds and indigestion*
9 Lemon balm *reduces anxiety and headaches*
10 Garlic *antibiotic; clears congestion and lowers cholesterol levels*
11 Comfrey *(restricted in some countries) leaf poultice for aches, burns, sprains, and cleaned cuts*
12 Ginkgo *tonic for cerebral circulation*
13 Sweet violet *leaf infusion soothes coughs*
14 Valerian *nature's tranquilizer; eases stress*
15 Lavender *relieves depression and headaches*
16 Red peony *root is used in Chinese medicine to ease eczema*

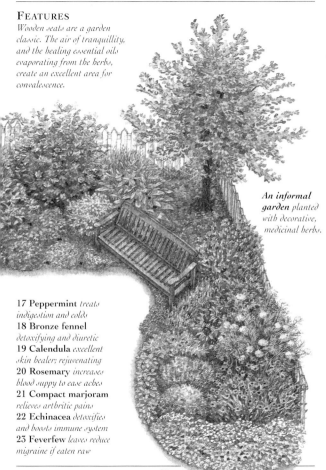

FEATURES
Wooden seats are a garden classic. The air of tranquillity, and the healing essential oils evaporating from the herbs, create an excellent area for convalescence.

*An **informal garden** planted with decorative, medicinal herbs.*

17 Peppermint *treats indigestion and colds*
18 Bronze fennel *detoxifying and diuretic*
19 Calendula *excellent skin healer; rejuvenating*
20 Rosemary *increases blood suppy to ease aches*
21 Compact marjoram *relieves arthritic pains*
22 Echinacea *detoxifies and boosts immune system*
23 Feverfew *leaves reduce migraine if eaten raw*

A Container Garden

Pot-grown plants can form an entire herb garden when space is scarce. This layout includes four minitheme designs in a trough, half-barrel, and pots. Pick and use leaves often to encourage new growth, keep neat shapes, and prevent top-heavy herbs from drying out. Reposition pots to catch the sun.

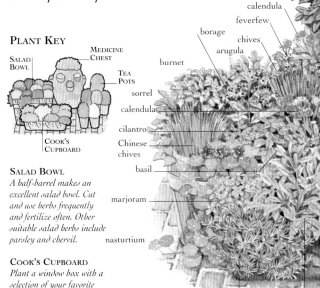

PLANT KEY

SALAD BOWL · MEDICINE CHEST · TEA POTS · COOK'S CUPBOARD

calendula
feverfew
chives
arugula
borage
burnet
sorrel
calendula
cilantro
Chinese chives
basil
marjoram
nasturtium
rosemary
sage

SALAD BOWL

A half-barrel makes an excellent salad bowl. Cut and use herbs frequently and fertilize often. Other suitable salad herbs include parsley and chervil.

COOK'S CUPBOARD

Plant a window box with a selection of your favorite culinary herbs.

MEDICINE CHEST
This strawberry pot has medicinal herbs. Wild strawberry, mint, and lemon balm are also useful.

TEA POTS
These individual pots hold a selection of leaf teas. They can be moved around easily or brought inside.

TYPES OF CONTAINER
Larger pots retain more moisture and allow a full season's growth. Insert a thin tube next to the herb to carry water deep into the pot.

aloe vera

purple sage

chamomile

thyme

golden lemon balm

sage

Moroccan spearmint

perennial chamomile

parsley
basil
tarragon
thyme
chives
peppermint
lemon verbena

Catalog of

GARDEN
HERBS

❖

*The following pages provide
a fully illustrated guide to 26
versatile and easy-to-grow
garden herbs. Each is listed
alphabetically by its botanical
name and is described in
detail to aid identification.
There is also information on
cultivating and harvesting
herbs, and tips on their uses.*

Allium species

CHIVES & GARLIC

These popular herbs belong to the
onion (allium) family. Chives are
a versatile flavoring and garnish;
garlic enhances savory dishes
worldwide. Both of the herbs have
important medicinal properties.

Chives: perennials
*24in (60cm) high,
12in (30cm) spread.*

CULTIVATION

Site: Sun or some shade.
Soil: Rich, moist, and
well-drained (pp.76–7).
Propagating: Sow seed
in spring; divide
garlic bulb or chive
clumps in autumn or
spring (pp.79, 84–5).
Growing: Transplant or
thin chives to 9in (23cm)
apart; garlic bulbs to 6in
(15cm). Water during dry
spells; fertilize soil
annually. Remove
flowers. Replant
every 3–4 years.
Pot in autumn for
indoor crop (pp.86–7).

A. schoenoprasum (chives)
*Globular mauve flowers in mid-
summer; long, hollow leaves have
a mild onion flavor.*

HARVESTING & STORING

Cut chive stems, leaving 2in (5cm) for regrowth. Freeze leaves, refrigerate, or dry. Pick chive flowers as they open. Dig garlic bulbs in late summer; dry (pp.90–93).

OTHER USES

Household: Chives deter aphids. Plant garlic near roses to enhance rose scent.
Medicinal: Sprinkle chives on food to stimulate appetite. Garlic is used to clear mucus and can help reduce cholesterol levels in the blood.

A. sativum (garlic)
Has white summer flowers, flat leaves, and a culinary bulb. Grows up to 39in (1m) high with a 6–9in (15–25cm) spread.

Long, flat leaves

Garlic cloves
A bulb is made up of 5–20 garlic cloves; its flavor increases the more it is sliced or crushed.

IN THE KITCHEN

Finely snipped chives go well with eggs, salads, soft cheeses, potatoes, and sauces.

When cooking with chives, add at the last minute to retain their delicate flavor.

Use garlic sparingly to enhance meat, seafood, and many vegetable dishes.

Both make good vinegar flavorings.

A. tuberosum
(Chinese chives)
Starry white flowers; flat green leaves have a mild garlic flavor.

Aloysia triphylla (Lippia citriodora)

LEMON VERBENA

This South American plant became popular worldwide for its perfume oil, once used extensively in cosmetics. Its immediate attraction lies in its leaves, which fill the air with a delicious, lemony fragrance.

Deciduous shrub with a height and spread up to 10ft (3m).

CULTIVATION

Site: Full sun. In winter a straw-covered, pruned plant that has deep roots should survive cold weather.

Soil: Light, well-drained, and alkaline. Poor soil produces stronger plants able to survive cold winters (pp.76–7).

Propagating: Sow in spring. Take softwood cuttings in late spring (pp.79, 82–3).

Growing: Thin or transplant to 39in (1m) apart. Prune any drooping branches to encourage new growth. Move indoors in winter. Prune and spray with warm water in spring to revive (pp.86–9).

Dried leaves
Excellent in potpourri, these retain their scent for 2–3 years.

HARVESTING & STORING

The leaves can be picked at any time, but lemon verbena is at its most fragrant when its flowers begin to bloom. Dry the leaves, keeping the pieces as large as possible to avoid loss of their volatile oil through exposure to air. Use fresh leaves to flavor oil and vinegar (pp.90–93).

IN THE KITCHEN

❖

Infuse leaves for a refreshing herbal tea.

Use as a flavoring for drinks, fruit desserts, and ice cream.

Leaves are tough and fibrous, so chop finely or remove before serving.

Aloysia triphylla
Has tiny clusters of flowers and long, pointed leaves.

OTHER USES

Household: Use dried leaves in potpourri, linen sachets, herb pillows; also to scent ink and paper.

Cosmetic: Soak cotton balls in a leaf infusion, then place over the eyes for 15 minutes to reduce puffiness. Make a floral vinegar to soften and freshen skin. Infuse leaves and add to bathwater.

Medicinal: Lemon verbena tea is mildly sedative and has a reputation for soothing abdominal discomfort and digestive spasms.

Anethum graveolens

DILL

Dill's uniquely flavored leaves and seeds are popular in Scandinavian and Eastern European cuisine. An important medicinal herb since biblical times, it also has excellent digestive properties.

Aromatic annual *up to 39in (1m) tall with a 12in (30cm) spread.*

Flowering top
Yellow flowers and green seed heads have the strongest flavor.

CULTIVATION

Site: Full sun and sheltered.
Soil: Well-drained (pp.76–7).
Propagating: Sow in spring until midsummer. Do not plant near fennel as it may cross-pollinate (pp.78–9).
Growing: Thin to 9–12in (23–30cm) apart (p.79).

HARVESTING & STORING

Cut leaves when young. Pick the flowering tops just as the fruits begin to form. To collect seed, after the flowering head has turned brown, hang the whole stem over a cloth. Dry or freeze leaves; dry ripe seed. Make dill vinegar from seed or flowering tops (pp.90–93).

Anethum graveolens
Aromatic, feathery, thread-like, blue-green leaves and a hollow, branching stem.

IN THE KITCHEN

❖

*Use flowering tops or seed in
egg, seafood, and potato dishes.*

*Add one flowering top per jar to
pickled cucumber.*

*Flavor and garnish meat or
fish with finely chopped leaves.*

Serve seed as a digestive.

Seed
*Aromatic, flattish,
oval; contains
some valuable
mineral salts.*

OTHER USES

Cosmetic: Infuse crushed seed
for a nail-strengthening bath.
Chew seed to sweeten breath.
Medicinal: Seed adds flavor
in a salt-free diet. A seed
infusion is good for hiccups,
indigestion, stomach cramps,
gas, and colic. Infuse ½oz
(13g) bruised seeds in ½cup
(225ml) boiling water.

Angelica archangelica

ANGELICA

This moisture-loving, bittersweet, aromatic plant was valued as a medieval panacea. It is most often used as a decoration for sweet dishes and to flavor gin.

Short-lived *perennial up to 8ft (2.5m) tall, 4ft (1.2m) spread.*

Leaves are large, glossy, divided and bright green

Thick, hollow, ridged stem

Angelica archangelica
Produces tiny, green-white flowers in its third year, then seeds and dies.

CULTIVATION

Site: Light shade. Angelica benefits from a mulch when it is in full sun.

Soil: Prefers deep and moist soil (pp.76–7).

Propagating: Allow to self-seed, or sow fresh in early autumn. Seed is unlikely to germinate when more than three months old (pp.78–9).

Growing: Transplant angelica seedlings in spring before the taproot becomes established. Leave a square yard/meter between plants. Not suitable as an indoor plant.

HARVESTING & STORING

Cut stems before midsummer for crystallizing. Harvest the leaves before flowering. Ripe seed should be collected in late summer. Dig up root in autumn of the first year. Dry leaves and root. Crystallize stems, wrap in foil, and store in a cool, dry place; do not refrigerate (pp.90–92).

IN THE KITCHEN

Blanch young shoots and add to green salads.

Stew leaf with tart fruits to reduce acidity.

Mix finely chopped fresh leaves with mint and mayonnaise.

Decorate cakes with crystallized stems.

Seed
Buff-colored seeds ripen in late summer of third year.

Crystallized stem
Choose fresh, young, pencil-thick stems; if brittle, soak briefly in warm water, then pat dry.

Dried leaves
These can be used to make a relaxing herb tea.

Dried root
This part of the plant retains its aroma the longest.

OTHER USES

Household: Use dried leaves in potpourri. A display of dried seed heads makes a striking winter decoration. **Medicinal:** Herbal tea helps to relieve bronchitis and coughs and acts as a general digestive remedy. **Caution: Avoid in pregnancy.**

Anthriscus cerefolium

CHERVIL

Chervil has a delicate, parsleylike flavor with a hint of myrrh and anise. One of the fines herbes, along with chives, parsley, and tarragon, chervil is indispensable in classic French cuisine.

Annual *up to 24in (60cm) tall with a 12in (30cm) spread.*

CULTIVATION

Site: Benefits from light shade in summer. In hot conditions, it quickly runs to seed.
Soil: Preferably light and well-drained (pp.76–7).
Propagating: The ripe seed germinates quickly; chervil is usable six to eight weeks after planting. For a regular supply, sow monthly except in winter. Scatter on soil and press in lightly (pp.78–19).
Growing: Thin seedlings to 6–9in (15–23cm) apart; avoid transplanting. Protect with cloches in winter. Will grow indoors with light shade and humidity (pp.86–7).

Dried leaves
These have little flavor, so use generously when cooking.

HARVESTING & STORING

Gather the leaves once the plant has reached a height of 4in (10cm), before flowering. The leaves are best used fresh but they can be kept for a few days in a sealed plastic bag in the refrigerator. Leaves can be frozen but their flavor does not withstand drying. Add lightly crushed leaves to vinegar (pp.90–93).

Anthriscus cerefolium
Has tiny white flowers,
fernlike, light-green
leaves, and a slender,
branching stem.

IN THE KITCHEN

*Small quantities of chervil
bring out the flavor of other
culinary herbs.*

*Add freshly chopped chervil
near the end of cooking to avoid
flavor loss.*

*Use leaf generously in salads,
soups, sauces, and vegetable,
chicken, white fish, and
egg dishes.*

*Sprinkle chopped stems in
salads, soups, and casseroles.*

OTHER USES

Cosmetic: A chervil leaf face
mask cleanses the skin,
maintains suppleness, and
helps to discourage wrinkles.
Medicinal: Leaf tea eliminates
toxins, stimulates digestion,
and helps to lower blood
pressure. It also alleviates
liver complaints and coughs.

Leaf is rich in
vitamin C, iron,
and carotene

Artemisia dracunculus

TARRAGON

Essential in French cuisine and used in savory dishes, tarragon's bittersweet, peppery taste has an undertone of anise. There are two types: the subtle, refined French and the coarser Russian.

Perennial *up to 39in (1m) high with a 15in (38cm) spread.*

CULTIVATION

Site: Sunny and sheltered.
Soil: Grows easily on rich, light, and dry soil (pp.76–7).
Propagating: Sow Russian tarragon in spring. Divide roots in spring. Take cuttings in summer. Divide and replant French tarragon every third year (pp.79, 82–5).
Growing: Thin or transplant to 12–18in (30–45cm) apart. Cut back in autumn. Protect in winter with straw or similar mulch. Can be grown indoors (pp.86–9).

A. dracunculus (French tarragon) *Has long, dark, narrow leaves.*

HARVESTING & STORING

Pick leaves any time, but in late summer for main crop. Sever a maximum of two-thirds of branch to allow for regrowth. Use leaves when fresh, or refrigerate for a few days, freeze, or dry at 80°F (27°C) (pp.90–93).

A. dracunculoides
(Russian tarragon)
Lacks anise subtleties and aroma, but improves the longer it grows in one place. Leaves are narrower and paler than French variety.

IN THE KITCHEN
✧

Use sparingly for a warm, subtle flavor.

Add chopped leaf to mayonnaise, salad dressings, light soups, chicken, and eggs.

Makes a delicious herb butter for vegetables, steaks, chops, and grilled fish.

Add to preserves, vegetable pickles, mustards, and vinegar.

OTHER USES

Medicinal: Infuse the leaves as a general tonic, appetite stimulant, and digestive.
Caution: Do not take this during pregnancy.

31

Borago officinalis

BORAGE

Borage is a native of Mediterranean regions and Asia Minor and has an ancient reputation for lifting the spirits and imparting courage. Its cooling, mineral-rich leaves have a refreshing cucumber flavor.

Annual up to 39in (1m) high with an 18in (45cm) spread.

CULTIVATION

Site: Open, sunny position.

Soil: Light, dry, and well-drained (pp.76–7).

Propagating: Sow *in situ* or singly in pots in spring for summer flowers; autumn for spring flowers. Borage self-sows on light soils (pp.78–9).

Growing: Set 12in (30cm) apart. Plant herbs near strawberries as they stimulate each other's growth. Tends to flop and might need staking: plant among roses for support, or prune in summer to keep tidy. Flowers attract bees to gardens. Small plants can be grown indoors (pp.88–9).

Seed
Largish, trisided, lozenge-shaped; often viable for up to eight years.

Leaf is rich in calcium, potassium, and mineral salts

HARVESTING & STORING

Pick the leaves in spring and summer when the plant starts to flower. Remove the flower heads by grasping the black stamen tips and gently separating the flower from its green back. Dry leaves; dry, crystallize, or freeze flowers in ice cubes (pp.90–93).

Borago officinalis
Has oval leaves on hairy stems, both of which are cucumber-scented when crushed.

IN THE KITCHEN

❖

Add young leaf and flowers to punch or Mimosa (a gin-based drink).

Decorate cakes with crystallized flowers.

Sprinkle flowers in salads.

Cook leaves with spinach, and add to ravioli stuffing.

Flower
Drooping, five-petaled blue stars with prominent black tips in the center.

OTHER USES

Medicinal: A leaf and flower infusion is a stress-relieving, antidepressant, adrenal gland tonic. Gamma-linolenic acid in the seed oil is good for eczema, rheumatoid arthritis, hangovers, blood pressure, and some menstrual irregularities. **Caution: Use the leaves in moderate amounts.**

Calendula officinalis

CALENDULA

Calendula (pot marigold) is a versatile herb almost constantly in bloom. It has been popular since ancient Egyptian times as a dye plant, for its cosmetic and culinary uses, and for its healing properties.

Annual with a *height and spread of 20–28in (50–70cm).*

CULTIVATION

Site: Sunny position.
Soil: Prefers fine loam but tolerates most soils, except waterlogged. Calendula does best during cooler seasons and should survive frost (pp.76–7).
Propagating: Sow seed outside in spring or singly in pots (pp.78–9).
Growing: Keep free from weeds and plant 12in (30cm) apart. Remove dead flower heads when necessary for almost continuous flowers and to prevent excessive self-seeding. Not suitable for growing indoors (pp.88–9).

Petals
Bright orange or yellow.

Dried petals
Keep their color well and have many uses.

HARVESTING & STORING

Pick flowers when open, leaves when young. Strip petals from flowers and dry at a low temperature to preserve color, or macerate in oil (pp.90–93).

Flower
*Up to 3in
(7cm) wide,
with petals
radiating
from center.*

IN THE KITCHEN

❖

*Petals give rice, fish, and soup
a light, tangy flavor.*

*Sprinkle tender leaves and
petals in salads.*

*Garnish meat platters, pâté,
and fruit salad with flowers.*

*Infuse petals to color dairy
products and cakes.*

OTHER USES

Cosmetic: Add the petals to
creams and baths to clean,
heal, and soften the skin.
Medicinal: Use infused oil or
cream for dry or inflamed
skin, dry eczema, and nipples
sore from breastfeeding. An
infusion stimulates the liver.
Calendula is antiseptic, anti-
fungal, and anti-inflammatory.

*Calendula
officinalis*
*Single or double
golden-orange flowers,
mid-green, hairy leaves, and
a succulent, branching stem.*

Carum carvi

CARAWAY

Caraway seeds have been found in the remains of Stone Age meals and are still widely used in central European cuisines. The aromatic seeds give a strong, nutty flavor to savory and sweet dishes.

Biennial *up to 39in (1m) tall with a 12in (30cm) spread.*

CULTIVATION

Site: Requires full sun.
Soil: Rich loam. Do not let soil dry out; the best plants are grown with continuous watering (pp.76–7).
Propagating: Can be grown from cuttings; is easily cultivated from seed. Sow outside in late spring or early autumn, in shallow drills in permanent position (pp.78–9, 82–3).
Growing: Thin seedlings to 8in (20cm) apart, when large enough to handle. Its long taproot makes transplanting difficult. Can be grown as an indoor herb if kept in a sunny position (pp.80–81).

Seed
Two narrow, brown seeds grow in each capsule. Use seed whole or ground.

HARVESTING & STORING

Gather leaves when young; use fresh. Dig up roots in the second autumn and cook as a vegetable. Pick seed heads in late summer or when seeds are brown. Snip stalks before seeds fall, tie in bundles, and hang the seed heads upside-down over an open container when drying (pp.90–92).

Carum carvi
Has tiny white flower heads and fine, feathery leaves.

Slender, furrowed stem

IN THE KITCHEN

✧

Sprinkle the seeds over pork or goose; use in goulash, and sauerkraut.

Seeds flavor pickles, cheese, cakes, bread, and cooked apples.

Add seeds to cabbage water to reduce cooking smells.

Serve raw or sugarcoated seeds at the end of a spicy meal to sweeten the breath and aid digestion.

Chop young leaves into salads.

Treat the root like a parsnip and cook as a winter vegetable.

OTHER USES

Household: Pigeon fanciers claim that tame birds will never stray if there is baked caraway dough in their cote.
Cosmetic: Use essential oil in mouthwashes and colognes.
Medicinal: Caraway is anti-spasmodic. Chew or infuse ripe seed to aid digestion, promote appetite, sweeten the breath, and relieve gas.

Chamaemelum nobile

PERENNIAL CHAMOMILE

The popular, daisylike chamomile is an ancient healing herb, still used for digestive and stress-related disorders. Its leaf gives off a sweet apple smell when stepped on and makes a fragrant lawn or seat.

Evergreen perennial
*up to 12in (30cm) high,
18in (45 cm) spread.*

CULTIVATION

Site: Requires full sun.
Soil: Well-drained (pp.76–7).
Propagating: Sow in spring.
Divide perennials in spring
or autumn; take cuttings in
summer (pp.79, 82–5).
Growing: Plant 4–6in
(10–15cm) apart for a
chamomile lawn.

***C.n.* var. *flore-
pleno* (double-
flowered chamomile)**
*Apple-scented leaves and
cream-colored double flowers.*

***C.n.* 'Treneague'**
*Nonflowering, mat-
forming; apple
scent.*

Matricaria recutita
(German chamomile)
*Annual with unscented foliage;
hollow-centered flowers have strong
honey scent. Plant 9in (23cm) apart.*

HARVESTING & STORING

Gather leaves any time; pick flowers when fully open. Dry both quickly (pp.90–92).

In the Kitchen

❖

Infuse flowers for a digestive, sedative tea, good for restless children, insomnia, and for suppressing nausea.

Dried flowers
Use these and dried leaves in potpourri.

OTHER USES

Household: Spray infusion on seedlings to prevent mildew. Grow near a failing plant to revive. Can be grown indoors.
Cosmetic: Used tea bags may reduce eye inflammation and fatigue shadows. A flower decoction lightens fair hair.
Medicinal: Valuable for skin conditions and irritations: apply a flower compress to eczema and wounds to reduce pain and inflammation.

Anthemis tinctoria
(Dyer's chamomile)
Golden summer flowers yield a yellow-brown dye when boiled. Not suitable for herbal tea.

Chamaemelum nobile
Flowers have golden-yellow centers and white petals. Creeping root-stock spreads plant, creating "carpet."

Light green ridged stem

Finely cut, bright green leaves have apple scent

39

Coriandrum sativum

CORIANDER/CILANTRO

Coriander has been cultivated for at least 3,000 years and is widely used in Middle Eastern, Asian, and Mexican cooking. The fresh leaf and ripe seed have very different aromas.

Annual *up to 28in (70cm) high with a 12in (30cm) spread.*

C. sativum
Loose, pale summer flowers; whole plant has pungent aroma.

CULTIVATION

Site: Thrives in full sun.
Soil: Rich, light (pp.76–7).
Propagating: Sow in autumn, to overwinter in a mild climate, or in early spring in final position. Grow away from fennel, which seems to suffer in its presence. Makes a good companion plant to anise as it speeds up the latter's germination and growth (pp.78–9).
Growing: Thin to 8in (20cm) apart. Coriander can be grown indoors, but some may find its scent unpleasant (pp.80–81).

Lower leaf is broad and finely scalloped

Lower leaf (cilantro)
Pungent aroma (same as upper leaves), but tastes like an aromatic parsley.

Root
Long, difficult to transplant. Cook fresh as a vegetable or add to curries.

In the Kitchen

❖

Add whole or crushed seeds to soups, sauces, curries, and vegetable dishes.

Fresh leaves flavor curries, stews, salads, chilis, and sauces – add at the last minute.

Use leaves as a spicy, fresh garnish.

Cook chopped stem with beans and soups.

Seed (coriander)
Small, round, and beige, with a light brown case. Sweet, spicy; hint of citrus.

HARVESTING & STORING

Pick young leaves any time. Collect seeds when brown but before they drop. Dig up roots in autumn. Dry the seeds; store whole, or infuse to make coriander vinegar. Freeze leaves, or place their stems in water and store in a plastic bag to retain their freshness (pp.90–93).

OTHER USES

Household: Use in potpourri. Seed essential oil is used to scent perfume, incense, medicines, and toothpaste.
Medicinal: Chew ripe seed or infuse as a tea for an apéritif, digestive tonic, and to relieve gas. Add the essential oil to ointments for painful joints and facial neuralgia.

Foeniculum vulgare

FENNEL

One of our oldest cultivated plants, fennel was eaten by the Romans to maintain good health and prevent obesity. Every part of the plant, from the seed to the root, is edible and has an anise scent and taste.

Perennial *up to 7ft (2.1m) high with an 18in (45cm) spread.*

CULTIVATION

Site: Full sun (to ripen seed).
Soil: Prefers well-drained loam. Avoid clay (pp.76–7).
Propagating: Sow outside in late spring to early summer (self-seeds when established). Divide in autumn (pp.79, 84).
Growing: Thin or transplant to 20in (50cm) apart. Do not grow near dill (p.24) or coriander (p.40). Remove seed heads (if not required) for better leaf production.

Bronze form
Has feathery pink, copper, and bronze leaves, with richest coloring in spring. Makes a ruby-red fennel vinegar.

HARVESTING & STORING

Pick young stems and leaves as required. Collect the seed when brown. Dig up bulbs in autumn. Freeze the leaves, or infuse in oil or vinegar. Dry the seed (pp.90–93).

Seed
Curved, ribbed, narrow, aromatic, and greenish brown.

IN THE KITCHEN

✦

Sprout seeds for winter salads.

Fresh leaves give fish dishes a delicious flavor.

Finely chop leaf over salads and cooked vegetables.

Add young stems to salads.

Slice raw bulb into salads or cook as a root vegetable.

Foeniculum vulgare
Has small, yellow summer flowers, lime-green leaves (dark green by autumn), and a round stem.

F.v. var. dulce
(Florence fennel/ finocchio)
A smaller version, grown as an annual for its bulbous rootstalk.

OTHER USES

Cosmetic: Chew to sweeten breath. Use seed and leaf in facial steams and baths for deep cleansing.

Medicinal: Digestives are made from seed. A seed infusion relieves bloating and stomach pains, aids digestion, and helps to increase nursing mothers' milk flow.

Laurus nobilis

SWEET BAY

A laurel wreath was a symbol of wisdom and glory in ancient Greece and Rome. Today, bay leaves are indispensable in cuisines around the world. Bay trees are also often grown as clipped potted plants.

Evergreen tree
*10–49ft (3–15m) high,
33ft (10m) spread.*

CULTIVATION

Site: Full sun or part shade. Needs protection from wind.
Soil: Rich, moist, and well-drained (pp.76–7).
Propagating: Take 4in (10cm) stem cuttings in late summer. Plant cuttings in a heated propagator with high humidity (pp.82–3).
Growing: Transplant to 4ft (1.2m) apart, in a frost-free area for the first two years (p.79).

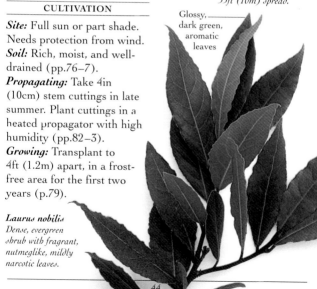

Glossy, dark green, aromatic leaves

Laurus nobilis
Dense, evergreen shrub with fragrant, nutmeglike, mildly narcotic leaves.

IN THE KITCHEN

*Bay leaf is a vital ingredient of
bouquet garni, used in stews,
soups, and sauces.*

*Add to marinades, stock, and
fish poaching liquid; boil in
milk for custard or rice pudding.*

Always remove before serving.

L.n. 'Aurea' (golden bay)
*Golden leaves; hardier than
the species when both are
small plants.*

L.n. 'Angustifolia'
(willow-leaf bay)
*Variety with narrow,
olive-green leaves.*

Dried leaves
*Use within a
few days of
drying for
the best
flavor.*

HARVESTING & STORING

Pick the leaves at any
time. Dry whole bay
leaves or branches to use
in herb infusions, powders,
and distillations (pp.90–93).
**Caution: All laurels except
sweet bay are poisonous.**

OTHER USES

Decorative: Clip the whole bay
tree into formal shapes.
Household: Crumble dried bay
leaves into potpourri.
Medicinal: A leaf infusion aids
digestion and stimulates the
appetite. Massage blended
essential oil around sprains
and into arthritic joints.

Lavandula angustifolia (L. officinalis or L. spica)

LAVENDER

There are more than 28 species of this fragrant herb, all with spikes of two-lipped flowers and small, linear leaves. Lavender essential oil, most concentrated in the flowers, has long been a valued perfume and healer.

Evergreen shrub with a height and spread to 39in (1m).

CULTIVATION

Site: Sunny, open position.
Soil: Well-drained and sandy with lime content (pp.76–7).
Propagating: Take 4–8in (10–20cm) cuttings, or divide, in autumn or spring. Sow seed in late summer and autumn (pp.79, 82–5).
Growing: Thin out or transplant to 18–24in (45–60cm) apart (12in/30cm for hedges). Remove faded stems; prune in late autumn and spring (pp.88–9).

Lavandula angustifolia (English lavender) *Small shrub with mauvish-blue summer flowers, narrow, fragrant, grey-green leaves and a square stem.*

Stem turns woody in second season

HARVESTING & STORING

Gather flowering stems just as flowers open. Pick leaves any time. Dry flowering stems by placing on open trays or hanging in small bunches (pp.90–92).

IN THE KITCHEN

❖

Flowers flavor jam, honey, sweets, vinegar, and tea.

Mix small amounts with other herbs for fragrant stews.

Crystallize for decoration.

Infuse flowers for a tea that reduces anxiety, headaches, nausea, and halitosis.

L. stoechas subsp. pedunculata
Magenta-pink flowers with purple bracts above and gray-green leaves.

L.a. 'Hidcote'
Compact, slow-growing; dark purple flowers, silver leaves. Makes a good hedge.

L.a. 'Munstead'
Small, early flowering, highly aromatic lavender with blue-green leaves.

L.a. 'Nana Alba'
Dwarf variety with white flowers; ideal for rock gardens.

OTHER USES

Household: Lavender sachets protect linen from moths. Use dried flowers in potpourri.

Cosmetic: Flower water benefits pimples or oily skin and helps to speed cell renewal.

Medicinal: Dilute essential oil is antiseptic and painkilling. Blend for use as a massage oil for ticklish coughs, joint and muscle aches, insomnia, and depression.

Levisticum officinale

LOVAGE

Lovage is a handsome plant with numerous culinary and medicinal uses, both traditional and modern. Its leaves, stems, and seeds give a strong beef and celery flavor to dishes, so add cautiously at first.

Herbaceous perennial
up to 6½ft (2m) tall with a 39in (1m) spread.

CULTIVATION

Site: Full sun or partial shade.
Soil: Prefers rich, moist, and well-drained soil (pp.76–7).
Propagating: Sow ripe seed in late summer (self-seeds easily). Take root cuttings in spring or autumn (pp.79, 82–3).
Growing: Thin or transplant to 24in (60cm) apart. Lovage is not suitable for growing indoors (p.79).

Levisticum officinale
Has large, dark green, celery-scented leaves and hollow stems.

48

HARVESTING & STORING

Pick the leaves as needed, but retain young central ones. Tie straw around young stems in spring to blanch; leave for 2–3 weeks, then harvest. Dig second- and third-season roots before flowers open. Gather seed when ripe. Freeze or dry leaves; dry seeds and roots (pp.90–93).

IN THE KITCHEN

Sprinkle seeds on salads, rice, or mashed potatoes.

Steep seeds in brandy for a settling digestive.

Toss shoots in oil and vinegar.

Leaves give body and aroma to soups and stews.

Dried leaves
Strong celery and yeast flavor; infuse as a broth or for seasoning.

Seed
Crescent shaped.

Dried root
This retains its aroma and is used medicinally.

OTHER USES

Medicinal: A seed, leaf, or root infusion helps to reduce water retention, eliminates toxins, relieves menstrual pain, and eases arthritic joints.
Caution: Avoid if pregnant.

Tiny, pale greenish-yellow flowers

Ridged stem

Melissa officinalis

LEMON BALM

Herbal writers have praised lemon balm's mood-elevating powers for centuries. Its essential oil is still used in aromatherapy to counter depression. The fresh leaves add a lemon tang to many dishes.

Perennial *up to 39in (1m) tall with an 18in (45cm) spread.*

CULTIVATION

Site: Full sun, midday shade.
Soil: Any moist soil (pp.76–7).
Propagating: Sow in spring; slow to germinate. Divide, or take stem cuttings in spring or autumn (pp.79, 82–5).
Growing: Thin or transplant to 24in (60cm) apart. Plant around beehives and orchards to attract pollinating bees. Cut back after flowering. Small plants can be grown indoors (pp.88–9).

HARVESTING & STORING

Pick leaves any time; handle gently to avoid bruising. Its flavor is strongest when the flowers begin to open. Dry leaves. Add fresh leaves to vinegar (pp.90–93).

IN THE KITCHEN

Chop finely into salads.

Add to white sauces for fish.

Float fresh leaves in plain tea, or infuse for melissa tea.

Try with sauerkraut, pickled herrings, poultry, or pork.

Leaves add zest to desserts.

M.o. 'Variegata'
(variegated
lemon balm)
*Gold-splashed leaves;
grow in light shade.*

OTHER USES

Household: Rub leaf on bee-hives before introducing a new swarm. Add leaf juice to furniture polish. Use leaf in potpourri and herb pillows.
Cosmetic: Infuse leaves for a facial steam and a hair rinse. Add leaves to bathwater.
Medicinal: Place fresh leaves directly on insect bites and sores, or apply in a poultice. Herbal tea relieves digestive problems, feverish colds, and tension headaches.

Melissa officinalis
*Has small, two-lipped,
late-summer flowers,
lemon-scented leaves, and
a hairy, light green stem.*

Mentha species

MINTS

Mints have been used as medicine and flavorings for thousands of years. There are over 600 varieties of mint, which continue to hybridize, so the best way to select a good plant is by nose rather than name.

Perennial 1–39in (25mm–1m) tall; indefinite spread.

CULTIVATION

Site: Some shade or sun.

Soil: Thrives in moist, well-drained, alkaline soil, rich in nutrients (pp.76–7).

Propagating: Take root or stem cuttings, or divide, in spring and autumn. Sow pennyroyal in spring (pp.78, 82–5).

Growing: Thin to 12in (30cm) apart, or transplant into large pots or plastic bags to restrain invasive roots. Mint can be grown in pots indoors (pp.86–9).

Oval, pointed, aromatic, wrinkled leaves

M. spicata 'Moroccan'
Moroccan spearmint has closely set, toothed, bright green leaves with a clean spearmint flavour.

M. suaveolens
'Variegata'
Variegated
applemint
has cream-edged,
mild leaves.

M. x *piperita* 'Citrata'
Fragrant eau de Cologne
mint is used in cosmetics
and potpourri.

M. x *p.* 'Crispa'
Crinkle-leaved black peppermint
has vibrant green leaves with
a strong peppermint scent.

M. pulegium
Creeping
pennyroyal
has bright green,
peppermint-
scented leaves.

HARVESTING & STORING

Pick mint leaves just before flowering. To preserve, dry, freeze, or infuse leaves in oil or vinegar (pp.90–93).

IN THE KITCHEN

❖

Infuse for an invigorating tea.

Use in mint sauce, syrups, and rich chocolate desserts.

Crystallize for decoration.

Add fresh spearmint or applemint to new potatoes, peas, fruit salads, and drinks.

OTHER USES

Household: Scatter pennyroyal in pet baskets and closets to deter fleas and ants.
Medicinal: Spearmint and peppermint are mildly anesthetic. Peppermint leaf tea helps digestion, colds, and influenza. For relief of colds, inhale vapor of dilute drops of spearmint essential oil.
Caution: Never take pennyroyal if pregnant.

Myrrhis odorata

SWEET CICELY

The attractive fernlike leaves of sweet cicely are among the first to appear in spring and the last to depart in autumn. Sweet cicely has a myrrhlike scent with a hint of anise, and is native to Europe.

Large perennial *up to 39in (1m) tall with a 4ft (1.2m) spread.*

CULTIVATION

Site: Light shade. Sweet cicely will tolerate sun.
Soil: Rich in humus; keep moist (pp.76–7).
Propagating: Easily grown from seed; sow outdoors in autumn since it requires several months of winter temperatures before it will germinate. Will self-seed once established (pp.78–9).
Growing: Transplant seedlings 24in (60cm) apart in spring. Sweet cicely will then benefit from a mulch of leaf mold and well-rotted manure or compost. Not suitable for growing indoors (p.79).

Unripe seed
Very large, green, ridged, ¾in (19mm) long. Edible, with a sweet flavor and nutty texture.

Ripe seed
Dark brown, glossy, ridged; use like cloves to add flavor.

Dried leaves
These retain a little scent and flavor.

Myrrhis odorata
Has small, white flowers, soft green leaves, a hollow stem, and a thick taproot with aromatic flesh.

HARVESTING & STORING

Pick young leaves any time; collect seed. Freeze or pickle unripe seed. Dig up root in autumn; peel and infuse in brandy (pp.90–93).

IN THE KITCHEN

◆

Sprinkle unripe seeds on fruit salads or ice cream.

Stir finely chopped leaves into salad dressings and omelettes.

Cook leaves with sour fruits to reduce acidity.

Add chopped leaves to cream for a sweeter, less fatty taste.

Toss roots in oil and vinegar.

OTHER USES

Household: Use crushed seeds to make a furniture polish.
Medicinal: The whole plant (but especially the root, when it has been steeped in brandy) is a tonic, a mild expectorant, and eases digestion. The leaf is a useful sweetener to help reduce sugar intake.

Ocimum basilicum

SWEET BASIL

This pungently aromatic herb has an intense clovelike scent. Tropical Asian in origin, basil has become an indispensable ingredient of Italian cooking. It is regarded as a sacred plant in India and in Greece.

Annual *up to 18in (45cm) tall with a 10in (25cm) spread.*

CULTIVATION

Site: Needs warmth and sun. Protect from wind, frost, and scorching.

Soil: Well-drained, moist. Grows well in pots in soil-based compost (pp.80–81).

Propagating: Sow seed in summer or indoors in late spring (p.78–9).

Growing: Water at midday; avoid overwatering seedlings to prevent mildew. In hot weather spray indoor leaves (p.89).

Ocimum basilicum
Has an upright, light green, branching stem and white, tubular, two-lipped flowers, produced on spikes in late summer.

Pointed, oval, bright green leaves up to 2in (5cm) long

HARVESTING & STORING

Pick leaves when young. Dry leaves or freeze (first paint both sides with olive oil); store in olive oil with salt or dry-pack with salt (pp.90–93).

O.b. 'Citriodorum'
(lemon basil)
Bushy habit, with narrow, oval, citrus-scented leaves; delicious with chicken and fish dishes.

O.b. 'Cinnamon'
Light pink flowers and a distinctive cinnamon aroma.

O.b. 'Minimum'
(Bush, or Greek, basil)
Dwarf, compact variety. Leaves have a milder flavor.

In the Kitchen
❖

Tear leaves to sprinkle over salads and sliced tomatoes.

Add torn leaves to pasta sauces and Mediterranean cooked dishes at the last minute.

Pound with olive oil, garlic, pine nuts, and Parmesan cheese to make pesto.

Use as a vinegar flavoring.

O.b. 'Purple Ruffles'
Frilly, deeply toothed purple leaves make this a decorative plant for pots.

OTHER USES

Household: Place pots of basil on a windowsill to deter flies.
Cosmetic: Infuse flowering tops and add to the water for an invigorating bath.
Medicinal: Steep a few leaves in wine for several days as a tonic. An infusion of basil leaves aids digestion.

Origanum species

MARJORAMS & OREGANO

These aromatic, spicy herbs are very closely related and similar in appearance, but sweet marjoram is less bitter. They are indispensable in Mediterranean cooking and also have valuable medicinal properties.

Perennial *up to 24in (60cm) high with an 18in (45cm) spread.*

O. onites
Pot marjoram has white/pink flowers.

CULTIVATION

Site: Full sun. Gold-leaf forms need midday shade.

Soil: Prefers well-drained, dryish, alkaline soil, rich in nutrients (pp.76–7).

Propagating: Sow seed in spring; take cuttings from late spring to mid-summer. Divide in spring or autumn (pp.79, 82–5).

Growing: Thin or transplant to 12–18in (30–45cm) apart. Flowers attract bees and butterflies. Cut back by two-thirds before they die down for winter. Suitable for growing indoors (pp.86–9).

HARVESTING & STORING

Pick young leaves any time.
Freeze, dry, or macerate the
leaves in oil or vinegar. Dry
flowering tops (pp.90–93).

O. majorana
*(sweet/knotted
marjoram)*
*Has sweet,
spicy leaves.*

IN THE KITCHEN
—✧—

*These herbs go particularly
well with tomato-based sauces.*

*Chop fresh marjoram into
salads or butter sauces for fish.*

*Add fresh marjoram in the last
few minutes of cooking.*

Rub on roasting meat.

OTHER USES

Household: Sweet marjoram
leaves are used in potpourri.
Medicinal: Sweet marjoram
tea helps colds, headaches,
and digestive and nervous disorders. Apply an antiseptic
oregano poultice to sprains,
arthritis, and a stiff neck.

O. vulgare
*Pungent oregano has
white/pink flowers.*

Leaves
contain
thymol, an
antiseptic

O.v. 'Aureum'
*Golden marjoram has
mild, savory leaves.*

O.v. 'Compactum'
*Compact marjoram has
dark pink flowers and
pungent, savory leaves.*

Petroselinum crispum

PARSLEY

Consumed in large quantities by the Romans, parsley is a beneficial and attractive herb. There are many varieties, all rich in chlorophyll, vitamins, and mineral salts.

Biennial *up to 15in (38cm) high with a 12in (30cm) spread.*

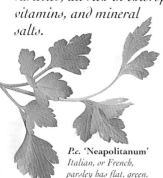

P.c. 'Neapolitanum'
Italian, or French, parsley has flat, green, strongly flavored leaves.

CULTIVATION

Site: Full sun or light shade.
Soil: Rich, moist (pp.76–7).
Propagating: Sow in spring to late summer. Slow to germinate. Self-seeds (pp.78–9).
Growing: Thin or transplant to 9in (23cm) apart. Protect in cold weather (pp.86–7).

HARVESTING & STORING

Pick leaves in first year. Will stay fresh for a few days in a plastic bag in the refrigerator, or sprinkle with water and wrap in paper towels; dry or freeze. Collect seeds when ripe. Dig up roots in autumn of second year; dry, or blanch and freeze roots (pp.90–93).

Dried leaves
Dry quickly to retain flavor; use in cooking. Boil with stem for a green-yellow dye.

IN THE KITCHEN

Use in bouquet garni.

Parsley enhances other flavors, but add near the end of cooking.

Flat-leaf parsley has the most flavor and is best for cooking.

Finely chop leaves and garlic; sauté. Add at the last minute to steak, fried fish, or vegetables.

Finely chop curled parsley and sprinkle over boiled potatoes as a garnish.

OTHER USES

Household: Grow by roses to improve their health and scent. Can be grown indoors.
Cosmetic: Leaf infusions are a tonic for dry skin and hair.
Medicinal: Chew parsley leaf to freshen breath. The leaf contains a compound that lessens allergic reactions and skin aging. A root decoction reduces water retention.
Caution: Excessive amounts of the seed can be toxic. Do not take during pregnancy or if you have kidney disease.

P. crispum
Curly parsley has finely cut, bright green leaves and a branching stem.

Succulent stem has strong aroma

Rosmarinus officinalis

ROSEMARY

Rosemary, "dew of the sea," is, for many, the essence of a summer herb garden. An aromatic, strongly flavored herb long used by cooks and apothecaries, rosemary also makes a good garden hedge.

Evergreen perennial
with a height and spread to 6½ft (2m).

Rosmarinus officinalis
Resinous, leathery, needlelike, dark green leaves; stem turns woody from second year.

CULTIVATION

Site: Sunny and sheltered.
Soil: Needs excellent drainage. On alkaline soil, it is a smaller but more fragrant plant. To make the soil more alkaline, apply eggshells or wood ash (pp.76–7).
Propagating: Grow indoors from seed in spring, outside in summer. Germination is erratic, needs at least 70°F (21°C) (pp.78–9).
Growing: Thin or transplant to 9in (23cm) apart. Protect in cold weather. Can be grown indoors in a sunny position (pp.80–81, 86–7).

R.o. 'Majorca Pink'
Clear pink flowers, bright green leaves.

R.o. 'Albus'
White flowers, occasionally with lavender veining.

R.o. 'Prostratus'
Prostrate species; has bright blue flowers.

R.o. 'Miss Jessopp's Upright'
White flowers, vertical growth; makes a good hedge.

HARVESTING & STORING

Pick small amounts all year round; gather main leaf crop before flowering. Dry sprigs and branches. Strip off leaves to store. Crush before use to release aroma (pp.90–92).

IN THE KITCHEN

Add sparingly to a wide range of meat dishes, particularly lamb and pork.

Infuse slow-cooking dishes with sprigs. Remove before serving.

Makes a delicious herb butter for vegetables.

OTHER USES

Household: Strip leaves and use stems to make barbecue skewers. Use in potpourri. Lay sprigs among linens.
Cosmetic: Infuse leaves as a rinse for dark hair.
Medicinal: Rosemary is a stimulant for the nervous system and eases arthritis pain. It is also an antiseptic gargle and mouthwash.

Rumex acetosa

SORREL

Prolific flowering stalks of sorrel can give a hay field a reddish tint at harvest time. Sorrel leaves are thirst quenching and most have an intriguing sharp, acidic flavor, used to advantage in many dishes.

Perennial *up to 4ft (1.2m) tall, with a 36in (90cm) spread.*

CULTIVATION

Site: (*R. acetosa*) Sun or light shade; (*R. scutatus*) Full sun in a sheltered spot.
Soil: (*R. acetosa*) Moist, rich with iron; (*R. scutatus*) Well-drained (pp.76–7).
Propagating: Sow seed in spring; germination takes 7–10 days. Divide roots in autumn (pp.78–9, 84–5).
Growing: Thin or transplant to 12in (30cm) apart. Water frequently. Divide and replant every 5 years. Can be grown indoors (pp.80–81).

R. scutatus (buckler-leaf sorrel)
Silvery patches on light green leaves, which have a sharp lemony flavor.

— Stem is juicy, ridged, and reddish

HARVESTING & STORING

Gather leaves when young for culinary use. Cover with cloches for a winter supply (p.87). Sorrel is best frozen for cooked dishes; dried sorrel has little flavor (pp.90–93).

IN THE KITCHEN
✧

Eat raw young leaves in salads and in sorrel soup.

Cook like spinach, changing the water once to reduce acidity.

Season vegetable soups, omelettes, lamb, and beef dishes with freshly chopped leaves.

Use in sauces for fish and pork.

Lance-shaped ——— leaves contain potassium and vitamins

R. acetosa
(broad-leaf sorrel)
Has whorled, reddish green flower spikes in summer; remove these to ensure a continued supply of young, succulent leaves.

OTHER USES

Household: Acid in leaf juice removes mold, rust, or stains from linen, wicker, and silver.
Medicinal: Infuse the vitamin-rich leaves to make a diuretic tea that alleviates some kidney and liver ailments.
Caution: Should be avoided by those with a tendency to develop kidney stones.

——— Acidity develops
as season
progresses

Salvia officinalis

SAGE

Sage is a powerful healing plant, and the name salvia, *from the Latin* salvere, *means cure. Its strong flavor can overwhelm other herbs, so it is best used by itself in cooking.*

***Evergreen shrub** up to 30in (75cm) tall, 39in (1m) spread.*

CULTIVATION

Site: Requires full sun.
Soil: Light, dry, and alkaline is best (pp.76–7).
Propagating: Grow from seed. All forms grow easily from cuttings (pp.78–9, 82–3).
Growing: Plant 18–24in (45–60cm) apart. Cut back after flowering, prune often. Replace every 4–5 years. Will grow indoors in a sunny position (pp.80–81, 88–9).

Salvia officinalis
Aromatic evergreen with mauve-blue, two-lipped flowers, gray-green, textured leaves, and a square, hairy stem.

HARVESTING & STORING

Pick sage leaves just before flowering. Dry leaves slowly to preserve best flavor and avoid mustiness (pp.90–92).

S.o. 'Icterina'
(gold variegated sage)
Leaves have a mild taste.

S.o. 'Purpurea'
(purple or red sage)
Strong flavor; use in tea for sore throats.

OTHER USES

Household: Scatter among linen to repel insects. Burn to deodorize cooking smells.
Medicinal: Sage is a digestive tonic and stimulant. It reduces sweating, soothes sore throats, and is a hormonal stimulant useful for menopause.
Caution: Avoid if you are pregnant or have epilepsy.

IN THE KITCHEN

❖

Sage combines well with other strong flavors – mix leaves with onion for poultry stuffing.

Cook with rich, fatty meats such as pork and duck.

Blend into cheeses or butter.

Dried sage is more powerful than fresh so use sparingly.

S. sclarea
(clary sage)
Biennial. Large, aromatic leaves and long-lasting spikes of lilac flowers.

Satureja species

SAVORY

Aromatic savory is one of the oldest flavoring herbs, and its peppery spiciness enhances the taste of all bean dishes. Savory has antiseptic properties, improves the digestion, and also acts as a stimulant.

Evergreen subshrub
up to 15in (38cm) tall,
30in (75cm) spread.

S. spicigera
Creeping
savory has tiny
white flowers
and deep green,
strongly
flavored
leaves.

S. hortensis
Summer savory
is an aromatic
annual with
lilac to white
flowers.

CULTIVATION

Site: Thrives in full sun.
Soil: Prefers well-drained, alkaline soil. Summer savory requires rich loam (pp.76–7).
Propagating: Sow seed in late spring or early autumn (sow summer savory in spring). Press seed lightly into soil. Take stem cuttings in summer. Divide savory in spring or autumn (pp.78–9, 82–5).
Growing: Thin or transplant to 18in (45cm) apart (thin summer savory to 9in/23cm). Prune established plants in late spring. Winter savory can be grown indoors (pp.88–9).

HARVESTING & STORING

Pick the leaves just as flower buds have formed. Collect the flowering tops in late summer. Dry the leaves and flowering tops. Infuse the leaves in oil or vinegar (pp.90–93).

IN THE KITCHEN

❖

Improves the flavor of legumes and all kinds of beans, even frozen or canned.

Add chopped fresh savory to horseradish sauce or mayonnaise.

Adds flavor to salt-free diets.

S. montana (winter savory)
Has tiny, pale summer flowers, aromatic leaves and a dense rootstock.

OTHER USES

Cosmetic: Use flowering tops in gargles, baths, and in facial steams for oily skin.
Medicinal: An infusion of flowering tops stimulates the appetite and eases indigestion. Steep tops in wine for a warming, stimulating tonic. Apply crushed leaves to relieve insect bites and stings.
Caution: Do not take during pregnancy.

Small, pointed, dark green leaves

Thymus species

THYMES

This highly aromatic native of the Mediterranean is one of the great European culinary herbs. Thyme is a valuable component of bouquet garni. *It also has powerful anti-septic and preservative properties.*

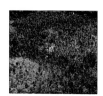

Evergreen shrub *up to 15in (38cm) tall with a 24in (60cm) spread.*

Aromatic, mid-green hairy leaves

T. vulgaris (common thyme) *Has pale lilac blooms; fine roots form a dense mat.*

CULTIVATION

Site: Plant out in full sun.
Soil: Light, well-drained, and alkaline (pp.76–7).
Propagating: Sow in spring. Take cuttings from spring to autumn; divide roots in spring or autumn (pp.78–9, 82–5).
Growing: Thin or transplant to 9–15in (23–38cm) apart. Prune frequently in summer. Protect in winter. Can be grown indoors (pp.86–9).

HARVESTING & STORING

Pick the leaves in summer. To preserve, dry, or make thyme vinegar and oil (pp.90–93).

IN THE KITCHEN

❖

Mix with parsley and bay in bouquet garni.

Add to stocks, marinades, stuffings, sauces, and soups.

Fresh thyme is very pungent – use sparingly.

Aids digestion of fatty foods.

Suits poultry, shellfish, and game cooked slowly in wine.

OTHER USES

Medicinal: Tea helps digestion and hangovers. Sweeten with honey for coughs, colds, and sore throats. Thyme oil is anti-oxidant and reduces cell aging, is antiseptic and anti-fungal. It also helps to relieve arthritis, muscular pain, and stimulates the body's immune system to fight infection. **Caution: Use oil in low dilutions; avoid in pregnancy.**

'Silver Posie'
Shrub with pale pink to lilac flowers and green leaves edged in silver.

'Fragrantissimus'
Shrub with pale lilac flowers and sweet, fruity, blue-gray leaves.

T. herba-barona
(caraway thyme)
Prostrate subshrub. Has rose flowers and caraway-scented leaves.

'Doone Valley'
Creeper with pale purple flowers, lemon-scented, bright green leaves with gold splashes. Delicious with chicken and fruit salads.

OTHER HERBS

There are many other herbs that are easy to cultivate and use. The following appear in the garden plans but do not have a catalog entry. Each is arranged alphabetically and has a brief description.

***A bed of** bright, peppery flavored nasturtiums.*

KEY

Abbreviations used: E = evergreen, P = perennial, Bi = biennial, An = annual, H = height, S = spread.

ALOE VERA *Aloe vera*
Long, fleshy leaves contain a healing sap and gel. Tender. E; H 12in (30cm), S indefinite.

BEE BALM *Monarda didyma*
Shaggy, scarlet blooms and fragrant flavoring leaves. P; H 48in (1.2m), S 24in (60cm).

COMFREY
Symphytum officinale
Curved clusters of mauve-blue, tubular flowers and rough, protein-rich, dark green leaves. P; H 4ft (1.2m), S 24in (60cm).

ECHINACEA *E. angustifolia*
Drooping, daisylike, purple to pink petals around a dark central cone; narrow leaves. P; H 5ft (1.5m), S 18in (45cm).

EVENING PRIMROSE
Oenothera biennis
Butter-yellow, night-scented flowers; long, pointed leaves. Bi; H 5ft (1.5m), S 12in (30cm).

FEVERFEW
Tanacetum parthenium
White, daisylike flowers and pungent, divided leaves. P, E; H 24in (60cm), S 18in (45cm).

GINKGO *Ginkgo biloba*
Deciduous tree with fan-shaped, notched leaves, gold in autumn. H to 130ft (40m), S 70ft (20m).

MADONNA LILY
Lilium candidum
Perfumed white trumpet flowers, lance-shaped leaves; bulb used in

medicines and cosmetics. P bulb;
H 5ft (1.5m), S 18in (45cm).

MEADOWSWEET
Filipendula ulmaria
Tiny, almond-scented flowers,
wintergreen-scented leaves. P;
H 4ft (1.2m), S 18in (45cm).

NASTURTIUM
Tropaeolum majus
Cheerful yellow-orange-red
flowers and round, edible leaves.
An; H 10ft (3m), S 6ft (2m).

PEONY *Paeonia officinalis*
White, pink, or red border
flowers. P; H and S 24in (60cm).

PINKS *Dianthus*
Fragrant white to red flowers. P,
E; H 20in (50cm), S 10in (25cm).

ROSES *Rosa species*
Fragrant flowers on shrubs and
climbers with thorny stems. P;
H and S to 15ft (4.6m).

SANTOLINA
S. chamaecyparissus
Mustard-yellow, button-shaped
flowers and silver moth-repelling
leaves. Useful as edging. P, E;
H and S 24in (60cm).

SOAPWORT
Saponaria officinalis
Single or double scented pink
blooms; oval, pale green leaves.
Produces saponin, a substance

that revitalizes old fabrics. P;
H 39in (1m), S 24in (60cm).

SWEET VIOLET *Viola odorata*
Sweet-scented, early spring
purple or white flowers. P;
H 6in (15cm), S 12in (30cm).

VALERIAN *Valeriana officinalis*
Tiny, pale pink flowers; leaf and
root smell of musk. P; H 5ft
(1.5m), S 4ft (1.2m).

WILD (ALPINE) STRAWBERRY
Fragaria vesca
Small, sweet, red fruit. Three-
part leaves become red and
aromatic in winter. E, P; H 10in
(25cm), S 8in (20cm).

SALAD HERBS

❖

ARUGULA
Eruca vesicaria Cream
flowers, peppery leaves. An;
H 39in (1m), S 8in (20cm).

GOLD PURSLANE
Portulaca oleracea Fleshy,
spoon-shaped leaves. An;
H 18in (45cm), S 24in (60cm).

SALAD BURNET
Poterium sanguisorba
Leaves taste of cucumber. P;
H 36in (90cm), S 24in (60cm).

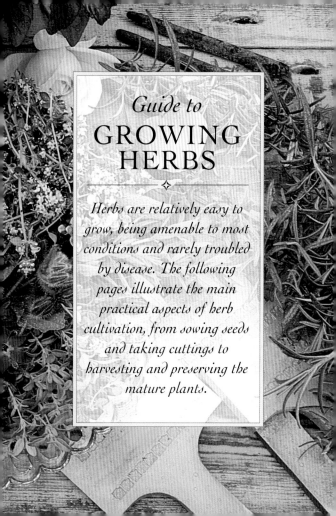

Guide to
GROWING
HERBS

❖

Herbs are relatively easy to grow, being amenable to most conditions and rarely troubled by disease. The following pages illustrate the main practical aspects of herb cultivation, from sowing seeds and taking cuttings to harvesting and preserving the mature plants.

PREPARING THE SOIL

Many herbs survive on poor, stony ground, but few can cope with waterlogged soil. Ideally, they prefer a light, open soil that is well aerated yet able to retain moisture and nutrients. To help herbs thrive, prepare the soil before sowing or planting in spring. Pot-grown herbs can be planted right away, but let soil settle for at least a week before sowing seed.

IMPROVING THE SOIL

To increase drainage and air in heavy soils, turn over in winter as frost helps to break down hard clods of earth. In early spring mix grit, horticultural sand, or vermiculite (a lightweight mineral) into the top 18in (45cm). If the soil is very waterlogged, dig a drainage ditch.

Fork over light soils in spring; remove weeds and enrich with well-rotted, straw-based manure or compost. Most herbs prefer a slightly alkaline soil; if yours is acidic, add a sprinkling of lime.

COMFREY FERTILIZER

Comfrey (p.72) makes an excellent fertilizer for poor soil. Loosely fill a container with leaves. Add water, cover, and ferment for 3 weeks. Dilute ⅓ cup (85ml) to 1 gal (1.5l) of water.

Organic fertilizer
Let comfrey leaves wilt for 48 hours, then dig into the soil as a green manure.

DIGGING THE HERB GARDEN

1 Avoid digging when the ground is too wet as this will damage the soil structure. Keep the spade upright, and do not load too much soil onto the blade.

2 Bend your knees as you lift the spade to prevent back strain. Turn over the soil to introduce air and incorporate compost. Dig up the roots of perennial weeds.

3 Break up any remaining clods of earth with a fork in spring and rake the soil smooth. When the first weed seedlings sprout, the soil is warm enough for sowing.

GROWING FROM SEED

Many herbs will grow from seed and readily self-seed once established. Chervil, dill, coriander, cumin, and parsley are best sown on site, but grow expensive or unfamiliar seeds indoors, where conditions can be controlled. When the seedlings are large enough to handle, transfer them to a bigger pot or tray and then plant out when spring frosts are over.

GROWING SEEDS IN TRAYS INDOORS

1 *Fill a seed tray with growing mixture; firm gently. Sprinkle seeds thinly over surface. Cover lightly with sieved soil mix, then water with a fine nozzle.*

2 *Cover with a sheet of glass to retain moisture, and with netting if in direct sun. Keep in a warm place. When seeds sprout, uncover but keep seedlings out of direct sunlight.*

PLANTING OUT

Herbs grown indoors need to be acclimatized before being moved outside. Set them in a sheltered spot during the day and take them in at night. Plant out after about a week, ideally in the early evening, when the sun is low and the soil warm. Select a site and water the soil. Make a hole larger than the pot and part-fill with soil mix. Remove the herb from its container (p.81) and place in the hole. Firm in with more soil mix. Note the eventual height and spread of each herb and do not plant too closely together.

SOWING SEEDS OUTSIDE

✦

Prepare the soil and sow annuals in spring, perennials in summer.

Using the side of a fork or hoe, draw a shallow, straight line about ½in (13mm) deep.

Sow seeds thinly, 2 or 3 per inch (2.5cm). Barely cover with soil; water with a fine spray.

Thin seedlings out when they are 2–4in (5–10cm) high.

3 *Once seedlings are large enough to handle, pick up gently by the leaves. Transfer into a bigger pot or tray to prevent overcrowding.*

GROWING IN POTS

Most herbs will grow in pots, but they need more care than those in the open ground. Pots are ideal for confining invasive herbs such as mints and can be repositioned to catch the sun or decorate a space. Most containers are suitable, provided they have drainage holes. Bring tender herbs indoors when there are signs of frost, and repot or replace the soil each year.

POTTING UP A CONTAINER

1 *Place a drainage layer of gravel, perlite, or broken crockery in the bottom of the container to prevent waterlogging. Fill with a soil- or peat-based potting mix to within 1in (2.5cm) of the rim.*

2 *Use a trowel or your hand to make a hole in the soil; the hole should be larger than the pot. Remove the herb from its original container (p.81). Set in the hole and firm in with more soil.*

POTTING ON

Herbs need transplanting into bigger pots when their roots protrude through the pot base. To remove, place a finger on either side of the stem, hold the pot base, and invert. Tap the rim against a hard surface to remove the root ball. Line a new pot with drainage material. Add some soil, then loosen roots. Put the herb in the pot. Fill with soil and water well.

GENERAL CARE

Clip or pick leaves often to encourage new growth.

Potted herbs dry out more quickly than those in the open ground. During hot weather check the soil every day.

Herbs with large soft leaves (like basil) need a fine spray to humidify air on hot days.

Feed every two weeks during the growing season with a weak liquid fertilizer.

3 *Plant up the container with a selection of herbs. Water well. Stand on a gravel-filled tray to drain. Fertilizer is unnecessary for the first 4 weeks. Move outdoors in spring or early summer.*

A strawberry pot (a large pot with several planting pockets) is an attractive way of growing a number of herbs together.

TAKING CUTTINGS

One of the most popular and reliable methods of propagating herbs is by taking cuttings. This ensures that the new plants will have flowers and leaves identical to those of the original. Cutting is also beneficial to the parent plants, which might otherwise become overcrowded and straggly. Propagate from healthy, vigorous herbs to obtain the best results.

ROOT CUTTINGS

During the dormant season, cut pieces of root about 3in (8cm) long. Insert in potting mix, making sure that they are the right way up. Use this method for herbs with long, fleshy roots, such as comfrey.

New roots form at the end that was farthest from the top of the parent plant

---

CARING FOR CUTTINGS

New cuttings need air, water, and warmth to enable quick root development, but keep them out of direct sunlight. When they show signs of growth, uncover and place in a sunny, sheltered spot but avoid hot midday sun. Fertilize and water when soil is dry (daily in summer).

After 4–6 weeks, gently pull a cutting to see if roots have formed (there should be some resistance), then pot up individually (pp.80–81). Grow on for about another month then transplant (p.79).

TAKING STEM CUTTINGS

STEM CUTTINGS
❖

This method suits bushy herbs such as lavender and rosemary. For the best results, take semi-hardwood cuttings (from new growth that has started to firm up at the base) between late summer and mid-autumn.

1 *Using pruning shears or a sharp knife, take cuttings from just below a leaf joint. Trim the stem, remove lower leaves, and snip off the top to encourage bushy growth.*

2 *Line the bottom of a pot with stones; fill with potting soil (p.80). Make a hole with a dibber and plant cuttings around the edge, to a third of their depth. Water.*

3 *Bend a piece of wire over the pot or plant three twigs around the edge. Cover with a plastic bag to retain heat and moisture. Open every few days to change the air.*

DIVIDING PLANTS

A cheap and simple way of restocking a herb garden is by plant division. This enables you to produce several healthy plants from one established clump, rejuvenate old herbs by cutting away dead growth, and also check their spread. Divide herbaceous perennials such as chives, lovage, and lemon balm every few years, or when they become too large.

How to Divide a Clump of Chives

1 *On a dry day in autumn or early spring, when the plant is dormant, ease out a clump of chives using a fork. Remove the old flower stems.*

2 *Shake the excess soil loose. Divide carefully by hand into pieces, each with a growing point and some roots. Discard unhealthy sections.*

3 *Replant immediately, in the ground or in pots (pp.79–81), so the roots do not dry out. Water thoroughly; cut back the top growth.*

4 *Place the plants in a sunny, frost-free place. Once they are about 4in (10cm) high, harvest regularly to maintain new growth.*

MOUND LAYERING

This method encourages new sections of a herb to grow while they are attached to the parent plant. It also improves the appearance of old plants, particularly sage and thyme, which can go woody in the center. In the spring, pile soil over the base of the plant until only the tips show. By late summer, new roots will have formed on many stems. Cut these stems off and pot up (pp.80–81), or plant in a new location (p.79).

To stimulate rooting, pile soil over the plant until only the tips are visible.

WINTER PROTECTION

Many herbs will not survive a cold winter outside, particularly when young. Bring pot-grown herbs indoors (if too heavy to move, wrap up in insulating material). Layer soil, straw, or mulch around the roots of mature plants. A large clear plastic bottle with the top cut off, inverted, makes an excellent cloche, a frost and snow cover.

BRINGING HERBS INDOORS

If brought inside and kept on a sunny windowsill, annuals live for a few months longer and less hardy perennials also benefit. Bring basil in at the first sign of crisp autumn air. Sage, rosemary, winter savory, and thyme will not survive long periods of cold. Trim roots that have grown through the base, or pot on (p.81). Transfer while the temperatures outdoors and indoors are similar, or use an unheated greenhouse for a few days to ease the change.

Insulate pots with burlap, bubble wrap, or newspaper.

WINTER PROTECTION FOR HERBS

1 *Lift the plants before the first frost and shake off any loose soil. Cut down stems to 4in (10cm) and remove leaves. Trim back roots to about 2in (5cm).*

2 *Half fill a 6in (15cm) deep box with soil mix. Put in the plants, making sure that they do not touch each other, then water thoroughly.*

3 *Store in a frost-free place until new shoots start to appear, then pot up the plants (pp.80–81). Use the new shoots as cuttings in spring.*

IN THE GREENHOUSE

❖

This is an ideal place to raise herbs out of season, or to protect tender ones in a cool summer. Chervil, parsley, and coriander will grow throughout the winter if sown in pots in early autumn (p.78). Divide clumps of chives, mint, and tarragon (pp.84–5), and pot up for winter use.

HEALTHY HERBS

Routine care, common sense, and observation are the main requirements for maintaining healthy plants. Herbs are mainly disease-free, but overcrowding in pots or too much water can weaken them. Remove dead flowers and leaves, and prune when necessary. Where possible, use natural methods to keep pests under control and avoid spraying herbs with chemicals.

Companion planting *French marigolds attract syrphid flies, whose larvae feed on aphids that attack nearby plants.*

ORGANIC CONTROL

When you buy or are given a new plant, plunge it into a bucket of mild dishwashing detergent to remove any insects that may lurk under the leaves. Hold your hand over the soil or cover it with plastic. Invert the plant, dip into the solution then gently swish around. Rinse in water.

The smell of certain herbs, such as mints and savory, may repel pests. Plant garlic and chives under roses to deter aphids. To combat persistent pests, spray herbs frequently with an organic or herbal pesticide.

Organic earwig trap *Fill a flowerpot with dried grass and place over a stake. Remove grass and discard every other day.*

MAINTAINING HERBS
✧

Control the growth of invasive herbs such as mints by putting in pots before planting outside.

Basil, tarragon, and marjoram grow bushier if the growing tip is pinched out (pulled off) first.

Remove no more than ⅓ of the leaves and allow time to regrow.

Prune lavender, rosemary, and sage after summer flowering.

Give herbs a substantial watering when dry rather than a little water more frequently.

Remove dead or damaged leaves and faded flowers.

PRUNING LAVENDER

1 *Using pruning shears, cut back dead flower stalks to 4–8in (10–20cm) of new growth in late summer or early autumn.*

2 *In early spring, cut back by 1in (2.5cm) to encourage new growth, making sure that some green shoots remain on the plant.*

HARVESTING & STORING

Fresh herbs are seasonal, but their flavors can be enjoyed year-round if preserved. Gather on a warm morning after the dew has evaporated, one type at a time to avoid mistakes in identification. Choose clean, healthy plants and handle gently. Use while fresh or preserve as soon as possible after harvesting, by drying, freezing, or infusing in oils and vinegars.

WHEN TO HARVEST

Leaves: Snip the whole stem of small-leaved herbs. For the strongest flavor, gather just before flowering.

Flowers: Pick at midday when fully opened. Snip lavender stalks; pick others by hand.

Seed: Collect when ripe (when they are no longer green), usually in autumn.

Roots: Dig up annuals in autumn; gather perennial roots in second or third year.

To avoid crushing and bruising, place herbs in a flat-bottomed basket, trug (below), or wooden box.

DRYING HERBS

Remove moisture gradually and keep herbs separate to avoid tainting.

Leaves: Hang stems upside-down in bunches. If drying small quantities of leaves, spread out on cheesecloth, net, or paper punctured with fine holes stretched over a frame. Keep in a warm, dry, dark place (an airing cupboard is ideal) and turn daily. At 75–90°F (24–32°C), leaves will dry in about 4 days.

Flowers: Hang lavender and other small flowers upside-down in bunches; dry as seeds. Will dry in 1–3 weeks.

Seed: Hang to dry over a box or sheet of paper, or with a paper bag or cheesecloth over the head. Will dry in 2 weeks.

Roots: Clean and cut roots into small pieces. Dry in a low oven, turning regularly, until they break easily.

Tie small bunches of about 5–10 stems together

1 *Small-leaved herbs are best dried on the stem in small bunches. Hang upside-down and dry in a well-ventilated place.*

Rub leaves off the stem when dry but keep whole

2 *When drying is complete, the leaves should be dry and fragile, but not powdery. Rub the leaves off the stems and discard the latter.*

DRYING FLOWER HEADS

Flowers should retain their color if dried correctly. Cut from stalks and place on a paper-lined tray; dry in the same way as leaves (p.91). Spread out delicate flowers to maintain their shape. When dried, store whole or separate the petals to reduce bulk.

Place calendula flower heads on a paper-lined tray, then let dry in a warm place for several days.

Thread chive stems through a wire mesh to suspend the flowers and keep their shape. Use whole as a garnish.

STORING DRIED HERBS

Store dried herbs in clean, dark glass, airtight bottles. Plastic and metal containers are not suitable as they affect the chemistry of a herb. Label bottles with the name and date. If condensation occurs, remove herbs and dry further. Check periodically and discard if there is moisture, mold, or insects. Most herbs deteriorate after a year. Put excess sweet-smelling dried leaves and flowers into potpourri or on an open fire.

HERB OILS AND VINEGARS

To make herb oil, loosely fill a clear jar with fresh herbs. Pour on unheated safflower or sunflower oil, cover with cheesecloth, and place on a sunny window sill. Steep for 2 weeks, shaking daily. Strain. For a stronger flavor, repeat with fresh herbs. Strain, bottle, and label. Follow this method for herb vinegars, using warmed cider or wine vinegar; cap with an acid proof lid. Strain, bottle, and label.

FREEZING HERBS

Freezing retains color and flavor, as well as most of the nutrients, and is good for delicate leaves such as chives and tarragon. Pack herbs into plastic bags and label. Store small packets in larger rigid containers to avoid loss or damage in the freezer. Alternatively, put finely chopped leaves or flowers into ice-cube trays. Add 1 tbsp (15ml) of water to each 15ml of herb, then freeze.

Freeze individual flowers and leaves in ice cubes to decorate or add flavor to drinks.

Borage flowers make colorful ice cubes

ADDRESSES

Canadian Herb Society
Van Dusen Botanical Garden,
5251 Oak Street, Vancouver, BC
V6M 4H1. Tel: (604) 922-5924

Richters Herbs
357 Highway 47, Goodwood,
Ontario LOC 1AO

Rosebud Herbs & Produce
RR 2, Olds, Alberta TOM 1PO

Forest Glen Herb Farm
County Rd 7/1 mile N. County Rd 12,
Forest, Ontario NON 1JO

Herb Garden
94 George Street, Oakville,
Ontario L6J 3B7

Stokes Seeds Ltd
39 James St, St. Catherines,
Ontario LZR 6R6

Vesey's Seeds Ltd
York RR, Prince Edward Island
COA 1PO

William Dam Seeds
P.O. Box 8400, Dundas, Ontario
L9H 6M1. Tel: (416) 6288-6641

ACKNOWLEDGMENTS

AUTHOR'S CREDITS
It is always a pleasure to work with
the clear vision and aesthetic skills of
a DK team. Special thanks to my
editor Sara Harper for her organized,
steady pace and good humor, and to
Liz Pepperell for her charming illustrations. A black orchid to Catriona
MacFarlane for her dry wit, and a
blue iris to Inka Hilgner for keeping
the herbs thriving. A red rose to my
youngest son Cameron Lowe for
emergency computer resuscitation
and a luscious bouquet of poppies
and sweet peas to my husband
J. Roger Lowe for everything.

DORLING KINDERSLEY
would like to thank Clare Marshall,
Claudine Meissner, Laura Jackson,
Lorraine Turner, and Nicky Vimpany.
DK Publishing, Inc. thanks
Irene Pavitt, Michael Wise, and
Phoebe Todd-Naylor.

PICTURE CREDITS
Key: t = top c = center b = bottom
l = left r = right

Photography by Martin Cameron,
Geoff Dann, Philip Dowell,
Steve Gorton, Peter Henderson,
Dave King, David Murray, Martin
Norris, and Steven Wooster, except:

Heather Angel/Biofotos 5, Clive
Boursnell 9bl; Deni Bown 9br, Eric
Crichton 8bl, 62tr; Garden Picture
Library/Linda Burgess 74–5, /John
Glover 1c, /Jerry Pavia 18–19; Clive
Nicols 6–7; Oxford Scientific
Films/Deni Bown 30tr, 64tr.

Illustrations: Liz Pepperell

Picture Research: Joanne Beardwell

DK Picture Library: Felicity Crowe